LAERTES IN AMERICA

Collected Poetry 2018-2020

LAERTES IN AMERICA

Collected Poetry 2018-2020

Stephen M. Honig

Design & Production by Jennie Hefren
Editorial Direction by Howard Wells

Printed in the USA

This volume is dedicated to every writer of poetry who dreamed that his or her spark might indeed set the topless towers of Ilium aflame.

Index

Author's Statement

This book is organized loosely around themes: America and its inherited ills; the rest of the world and its inherited ills; the healing nature of nature; my consideration of myself; my relationship with family and deity; my relationship with mortality. These themes roiled me these past few years, and you are burdened here with the detritus born of that process.

Two of the within poems were kindly included in *Ibbetson*, a poetry magazine generous enough to encourage my efforts. One was set to song by a friend of mine whom I have known since I was three days old—another story for another time.

Many of these poems are not pretty. Some I have been told are not poems at all, but rather essays with broken lines or screeds of improvident motivation. I have exercised the prerogative of the author to include what lies herein; it is for the reader to decide if this is poetry at all and, if not, whether that matters.

Having never published a book before 2019, I have been troubled by my sudden impatience; this volume is my fourth book of poetry in three years. It is indeed true that I feel in an enormous hurry, so much so that my wife likely is wondering if I am hiding some terminal disease that forces acceleration of publication.

I simply share the terminal disease of all of us, the years we live. Each of us is given a stack of chips for the poker game of life. When the stack is consumed, the game ends. The problem is that someone has dumped our chips into an opaque box; you don't know when the last one is being played until it is, by definition, too late.

January, 2021

I

AMERICA

Laertes in America

Laertes took a stroll through America.
Every time he thought he had found a son
he ended up alone with a long row to hoe.
He lacked foresight of his future,
And then succumbed too soon for it to matter.

There was not much familiar for Laertes
on his odyssey but,
of a sudden,
certain things rang true:

Chaos and pain and confusion
set on a disquieted stage,
where the script was ad-libbed
and people died with regularity.

A poisoned sword tip wavers over us.
You also know
that such poisons that go around
come around.

Pledge

I pledge allegiance
to the country
where my feet are burrowed in its mud
up above my ankles
deep in history and pain.
Mixture of earth and blood and tears
beneath unseeing eyes and skies
while people starve and bleed
flag waving
and a green statue stands mute
beside the bolted door.
Whose country 'tis of thee
where oceans dare but people fail
to climb up on our shore?

54

Robert Gould Shaw led the all black 54th Regiment in the Civil War. Author Robert Rosen wrote of him: "Robert Gould Shaw was buried by the Confederates on Morris Island, with the dead of his regiment, or, as the Southern press described it, in a ditch 'with his niggers.' Northern reaction was vehement, and many insisted Shaw's body be buried with dignity elsewhere. Shaw's father, however, wrote General Quincy Adams Gillmore, the Union commander, that 'a soldier's most appropriate burial-place is on the field where he has fallen.' "

Hard to picture.
Who can know the nature of things
one hundred fifty years ago
in the midst of war?

He died on the parapet of a fort that would not yield,
and the dirt of the ditch yielded for him,
tossed face-down into the sand, rotting flesh with rotting flesh
skins black and white
and all the same.

We cannot understand war by numbers,
or by trodding battlefields
or by reading of sorties and death.

We can only understand war
by digging into sand in front of Fort Wagner
to find bones of people whose skin color cannot be discerned.

Killer

He was a cook with an AK 47 and big plans.
He was a student in a dorm room chosen because its state had
lax gun laws.
She was a mother who blew away her children and herself.
He hated schools, or was it children, or was it his friends.
He sniped two teens who wandered on his property.
He shot up a nightclub.
He shot up a street.
He shot at random and killed a teenager of promise.
He shot at random and killed a little girl whose promise was
yet to come.
He killed for his gang.
He killed for his pride.
He killed for his family.
He killed because of his cat although his dog told him not to do it.
He killed in war and it became a habit.
He killed because he was fired.
He killed because he was not hired.
He killed because he was not promoted.
He killed her with a knife with her new masters in her pocket.
He killed because everyone needs a hobby.
He killed because of his race.
He killed for the art of it.
He killed for his President.
He killed for his religion.
He killed because she wore a scarf.
He killed because they wore skull caps.
He killed because it was an initiation.
He killed because of their color.
He killed because they were gay.
He killed because he wanted their sneakers.

He killed because he wanted to die.
He killed because he was high.
He killed because he was depressed.
He killed because he was nuts at that moment.
He killed because God made him do it.
He killed because speed made him do it.
He killed because he was allergic to coffee if it had caffeine.
His killed his father because he had it coming.
He killed because you slept with his girl.
He killed because you slept with his wife.
He killed because she slept with his team-mates.
He killed because they were going to deport him.
He killed because they were going to deport his kids.

He doesn't need no god-damned reason to kill and what's it to
you?

Sonnet for Terrance Hayes

You are black like I am Jewish.
Only different.
Different pains and different perceptions of pain.
Where one stands is the only unmovable point.
We both get lost in the rhythm of words.
We both get lost in the injuries of life.
You box your pain in fourteen lines.
Is it to make it yield to analysis?
Is it to seek your catharsis?
Or is it to control your own pain
as if more than fourteen lines hurts too much?
My pain would need four pages, but
I will limit myself here to fourteen lines,
just this once.

II

THE REST OF THE WORLD

Dust Bunnies

My mother called them dust bunnies,
Filmy gray and small bundles of dirt
Held together by hairs of no known color;
They lived under beds and chairs
And came out to play when carried by unseen household breezes,
Skittering elusively across polished wooden floors
Until, spied by mother,
They were scooped up by cloth or tissue
Or anything expedient
And dropped with mild distain into the trash.

Leon was a boxer of modest skill
An undercard sort of guy.
He trained in a nondescript gym on Livonia Avenue
Hard by the subway trestle
On the second floor,
Over a furniture store.
He was assigned locker number 104,
A gray box suffused with hints of rust
From dried sweat of Leon and his many predecessors,
And in the corners were dark accumulations of dust
Held in place by the oily remains of human exertion.
The perspiration carried by his shirts and shorts
Migrated to the corners to be absorbed by the hardened globs of dirt.

Roberta did not like the old age home
And the feeling was mutual.
Before the time where correctness told us to rename such places
As retirement communities or some other disguised nomenclature
Roberta sat in the narrow black rocking chair in her shared room

And watched the dust strands hanging from her ceiling,
Waving in tendrils supplied by spider webs sprung free to sway
And gather onto their sticky surface the floating motes of dust
That blew in the windows
Borne on winds sweeping the city streets below.

The parson suggested often
In his dour way
That ashes went to ashes and,
Well, you know don't you,
The tired refrain
Of dust to dust,
As if dust were an end-point of a journey which
May have enjoyed its high-points
But ended in pain and dirt.
He did not notice
That the final dust was everywhere in our lives,
Precursors of final times
Scouting our bodies to identify the texture and composition
Of that particular dust that was to be our eternity.
The dust of past lives,
Particles of all who came before
And returned to the ether of beginnings.

I cup the dust bunnies that flit across my floors
In gentle palms
And turn them loose out my back door into my garden,
Bidding my ancestors a place among the flowers.
I am not sure who they are
But I honor them all the same.

(Published in *Ibbetson, Vol #47)*

Wolf—for the three little pigs

Doors implode.
Thatch and wood fly.
Roofs rise to shade the sun.
And finally bricks
unmoored from mortar
shoot lethal arrows.
Foreboding etches on every snout.
Saliva drips from every pointy mouth.

I, destroyer of hubris, bringer of truth,
begin:
ham and hocks and ribs and bacon and chitlins and sinews
and brains and lungs and knuckles
and bristles descend into gullet
with a curled tail chaser.

The moral of this fairy tale is [pick one]

- a Boy Scout is always prepared but the porcine Troop forgot the message
- never jest at the dawn with death
- the road less taken leads to a jurisdiction with more robust building codes
- none of the above; morals are a false construct.

Le Parc de Plaisir

Flat foot floogie lost her floy
one day
on its way
to find its censored roots.

This is how it started.
This is how it will end.

No one sings the song
  anymore.
Young people, I am told, do not relate.

Some will go on trips
to Europe or their minds.
Though today, not so much.

In Paris, there is a carousel you must pedal.
Unfortunately, it travels only in a circle.

Hunter Bought the Ticket

He hung by the ultimate thread,
hands bloodied as the wire of his life
cut him skin and flesh to the bone
and then passed on through,
rendering him particles unwhole,
unwholesome and random,
in the eye of a mind he no longer controlled.

Corkscrews reamed and drained him,
even as their torque excited him,
as the w(h)ine drained into a glass with no bottom.
His ticket was punched twice
when only one fare was due,
and the price too high to start with.

His father once told him: when on the wrong side of the grass
there will be no answer to your question.

Time

Time is folding inwards.
Trapped in the seam,
the walls of history drop their detritus upon us.
We are dodging falling mastodons,
Ghosts of tyrants ancient and anew,
cities long burned,
cities yet unbuilt,
ambitions and insinuations.
We are stepping around and over the past.
We are stepping around and over the future,
Our running is of no help
or solace.
We are taunted by history not touching our bodies
but incessantly assailing our memories.

Here is the Thursday my father died
when the doctor said I should pull the plug.
Here is Ba'al in a basket with Moses.
Here is an army at the Rubicon, and another at Shiloh.
Here is a death march somewhere,
is it China, Bataan, The Trail of Tears, there are so many
now falling in a jumble like blood-soaked hail.

Do not step on a butterfly
as I have heard that the past is the future.

I see her eyes reflecting in flickering light,
her body caked in sweat.
I see his grave-stone atilt,
evidence of vandals or failed escape.
I see people of different breeds in coitus on savannahs,

I see children slaughtered in caves,
philosophers slain by churls,
priests burning women,
I smell their charring flesh,
I am in Philadelphia overlooking the Ganges,
and here is all hominid history,
each man a weapon in his hand.
Soft wafting hours and eons
melt them all before me,
dying in sequence and at random,
conveyed away by beasts and subway cars
into timeless dimension.

You are there to no avail,
your waving arms are lost in Brazilian jungles.
Souls shower onto the land
but the land is arid and nothing grows.
It is all good in the end
and, things being evil and thus not good,
we therefore are not at the end,
and we surely are not at the beginning
and thus we are the middle,
awash in all of time.

The sun will explode in flames; there still is history on this dying ember.
The sun will freeze and congeal; there still is history on this dying iceberg.
Atoms cease to buzz,
frozen electrons riding the haunches of saber-toothed tigers.
Helen of Troy lies down with Tiny Tim
while her towers burn in a different crevice.

We were told that time was linear
which was correct until it was wrong.
We are told that time is different,
that time itself has history,
that time itself occupies space.
I was reluctant to believe but
today
I have become an acolyte.

HOLD ME HOLD ME HOLD——
The blood of my finger-nails drips off the cliff edge
onto sailing ships,
gas masks,
hysterectomies,
wedding bouquets,
A girl slit in two on an altar,
A circumcision with knife lost,
Animals self-impregnating with rictus in their faces.

Is time a hill of sand sliding hourly in the wind?
Is wind the sliding sand through the hourglass of time?
Did they know we would end this way?

Careful! Do not cross in front of the elephant.

I had planned an epiphany for tomorrow
but tomorrow has passed over the horizon.
We had thought history to be linear and
we were correct until we were not.
My epiphany must wait until the future.
My epiphany happened long ago.

Life Explained

Pygmalion held his ivory, and
    upon transformation,
marveled at its morphology.
The gods seized the didactic moment
to explain:

Life is merely illusion,
    temporary suspension of an orthological world,
allowing planes and vectors
to exist for an instant, together, until
from the very beginning they were gone . . .

Speaking of Which…

We start here
    by definition.

We end in another place.

In between we call that life
    for want of a better word.

Do you ever find yourself sliding sideways?

If not, was it because you were not,
    or just failed to notice?

Is the search for purpose pre-ordained
    or self-inflicted?

When on a journey
    (which is just a road-trip with pretensions)
I think I am going somewhere
even when standing still.

The Racer

Mario Andretti awoke one night,
sat up in a mist of sweat,
recalling that his whole life was about going as fast as he could
but always in a circle.

At that moment, a sense of futility created vast emptiness.

Mario decided to admire his mobius strip
and fell back asleep without doubt or care.

A true professional knows how to get his rest.
There is always another race to be run tomorrow.

I Reached Out

I reached out
  to you
  you know, but
you did not seem to care.
I knew you felt my mind touch yours
  but coarser contact was your style.
I am willing to beg to have you
  but you know that, also, yes?
You know everything on this page
  except me.
Hair lust cringe and strut
  a life of dying flowers
  all on offer.
Your credit is good at my counter;
  your currency converts to heat at favorable rates.
My hand is dust
  blowing in your exhalations.
Drip blood and laugh at me, will you?
I taste iron in the air … essence of rust and playing cards
  pretending to be Tarot.

Love Takes a Ride

Love leaves by the front door,
riding on one harsh word too many
that cannot be retrieved.
Love leaves by the back door,
pulled by unrequited desires
that need to be bound in mystery.
Love leaves up the chimney,
incinerated by too much fire,
the hearth consuming all the home.
Love leaves through an open window,
a careless error encountering
a wandering heart.
Love is a random wanderer,
by bus or car, or by train or train of thought
without known destination,
but love can wander far
and never find its way back
and is said to have been lost.
Love itself demurs, for it is in motion,
in endless quest for new homes.

When you find a love on offer, ask yourself,
is it newborn or merely on the road?

Drawbridge

On the highway
the bell rings urgently; the draw-bridge will make way
for someone else's tomorrow.
Will the bridge come back down in time?
Is your future racing ahead too quickly?
Will you be distracted this side of tomorrow,
sucked into unexpected hallways
through random doors which do not lead you forward?

What if you hurry? Accidents occur when hurrying
and there is no assurance you will beat the bell.
Your future can be anywhere,
The bell may presage nothing.

The bell has ceased.
The road has risen.
Your destiny has decided your future.

Bridges and Options

One
There are bridges
A life of bridges
Can't hardly go anywhere but there's a bridge.
You got your old age bridge and your young age bridge
And love
    (maybe more of a tunnel
    or two)
    and sex which is different (God knows!).
Money
Respect
Some bridges hurt
    rough pavement
    falling off the edge
        without a bottom.
Strange are bridges:
Going onto one is all uphill and then when you hit the top
    it's uphill only steeper.
Looking for a woman who's on level ground
    even keel
    on the center line
    as I've tipped over the side of some bridges on my way
    and there isn't any bridge for the falling…

Two

Everyone's got a highway
    and no one has good maps.
Learned to avoid the bridges, for sure
    but then there's the old joke that you can't get there from here.
'Course, if you're going nowhere
    lack of maps isn't a problem.
Just make it up as you go along.
The latter, that's my plan
    if you can call it that.

Three

We have been informed there are tunnels
    for those who are feeling low.
It is dark and, where to go?
Life is beginning to seem complex when simple was my first choice.
You can live the high life, take the low road, or get lost trying to keep it simple.
Greeks recommended the middle ground
    but moderation and a quarter gets five nickels in this man's world
    and then only if you're lucky.
Show me a man who is wealthy
    and I bet you he never gets involved with bridges.

Four

I am staying right here.
I am looking at flowers, right up to my eye,
    pollen weights my lids and fills my nose,
    and there is music to be heard
    with pounding butterfly wings
    if you listen hard enough.
May I list the colors for you that I see?
On second thought, things are brighter if imagined
    and you can do that in your chair
    your garden
    your mind.
From my hill, I see the roads and bridges filled with cars
And the tunnels cut into the mountain.
They suggest to me disquiet and, perhaps,
a poem.
For later, perhaps.
I am, for now, quite busy…

Epiphany

Reader's choice.

Four a.m.

There is something about Four a.m.
that makes you think.
There is the foretaste of morning
mixed with the dream of unfinished fatigue.
It is not the depth of three which is an interruption of night.
It is not the quickening dawn with sun on its cusp.
There is a perfect fourness to Four a.m.

Welcome to Jerusalem

I am swathed in ambient slime
dripping from holy promises,
poured by willing acolytes who
know not what they do.
The train coming towards me has no rails
but its aim is true.
It will pass right through me as does every affront today
for today is a holiday from sins original and contrived.
People are talking about me, you know,
the light bulbs are burning out,
the black curved filament rattles in the glass,
the base is blackened by unknown fire.
It is not only trite to claim to be sinking,
it is also far too late.
Amazed am I beneath all of life
that visibility is so clear
but the path is so hidden.
I would complain but all I ever get is assurance
that my call is very important to the recipient.
I suspect all recipients share a chasm into which
    important calls are placed
carefully and catalogued
so as to be sure that, if repeated,
they shall not be answered.
Atoms slide past me,
their electrons leaving palpable traces in the substance
    of space
at different places also
as that is science, and who am I to argue?

I thought love would save me and it did
for a while
but all things decay,
haven't you heard,
the best ones faster
as they absorb the friction of use.
There is an end to this story
but it is not a story so perhaps not.

Topless Towers Aflame

They are long dead
if they lived at all.
Dead in the world and in their myth.
They were slain by men and by gods,
by sword and by arrow,
by being flung from parapets,
by being tricked by a large wooden horse,
by rape and by fire,
by plunder and by treachery,
so they could not inherit thrones,
so they could inherit women,
because they were as beautiful as Helen,
because they were as fierce as Paris,
because they fell on their own lances
or because they could not find them.

Their City was found half a continent away from history.
Their heirs spread across Italy.
The heirs of their heirs salted Carthage as she burned.

They are confused by poets,
confounded by playwrights,
debated by professors,
cursed by students,
unrequited by archeology
and unremembered by all but those who care for such things.

She slept with many men,
some husbands and some not.
The armada of a thousand ships not enough to keep men away
who lusted at the cost of their souls.
They are, as all of us, flotsam washed ashore by the ages
in unbreakable tangles,
words and names and hillocks covering stones of something we
do not understand.

And thus we come to ourselves,
searching still for who we are,
by asking who they were,
three thousand years ago…
or not at all.

Victoria in the Morning of My Leaving

Victoria sat up in bed.
Buzz-saws whined and she
was not fully enlightened.
A failure of will.

Light falls but shadows persist.
Anomalies abound.
Forests hide things we do not need to know.
It was Thursday, I recall.

Time is future.
You know that.
Lines of biblical import verged and
fell on end to no end.

Breakfast eggs sat cold
in congealed bacon fat
on that long ago
tomorrow.

West is the direction of salvation.
Some head East.
The literati head South
which is their failure.

I was pure last year
but it did not work out.
I used my options and now
my bespoke clothes are no longer in style.

You can work it out in wood.
Ask Victoria for her saw.
It was Thursday
and I was heading South.

Feral in the City

Some say it is hard to be feral in the City.
They do not understand.
Things are confused in the City,
right and wrong all mixed up.
People are so careful about themselves
that they forget to be careful about their neighbors.
Friends are diluted by density.
People see themselves as smart and sophisticated.
People rely too much on the police
or they do not involve them at all.
Self-delusion from confusion.
Laxity in the presence of risk.

I love the poor.
I love the old.
I love the stupid.
I love the self-righteous,
the self-inflated.
the over-confident.
Those who are dope, hip, woke, cool.
The fools invent names for themselves
to feel not alone.
I love the main chance,
all the losers lined up dumb as a rock,
pillage by force not needed,
concentrated herd of marks,
all packaged up for me block by block,
natural selection on parade.
I employ them and rape them.
I tax them and take them.

I kill you and suck your marrow.
I fuck you and suck your nipples.
I dominate you, as I am advised to do.
My banker thinks you are scum
and red-lines you unto the fifth generation.
I am judge of the jungle,
top man of the tenements,
boss of the Bowery,
guru of the ghetto,
and by the way,
I own you and you don't even know it.

I am lord of you and all you borrow
for you don't own anything.
I enjoy you as you wallow in sorrow
begging for something.
I own your children and your tomorrow,
and you are nothing.

Hear me roar—
Feral in the City.

I Was Born in 1810

In 1891 or so
hard to remember sometimes
the root entered my box and began to suck on me
drawing what little moisture I had absorbed
and I could feel the minerals ascend.
Then more roots, many more roots
digging through me and dissolving me
on their way deep into the hillside
until I was all ascended
not to heaven
but in branches and deep dark pine needles.
It was thrilling to find myself in wind and snow and rain
and warming heat
being dead in 1824 at such a tender age
of the fever I assume
though no one told me so.
And in the air I could see the horses cede the converging roadways
to the mechanical devices
and the people changing in dress and language
yes a glimpse of the future denied to many in the old cemetery.

The tree is now well over 100 years of age
and that is exciting to think about
as I can assure you that your body has no such prospect
unless luck will have its way
and you can grow brown and green and tall
through osmosis of body and soul.

Today a young child came and
made a picture of the base of me.
My trunk is deep brown-black in color
with etched runnels vertically striping my leg, which

has slowly enclosed the stone which my mother had set
two centuries ago
so that people could remember me
though so many died so long ago that soon no one came to
 remember.
The wind mercifully wore away my name
a suitable act I tell you
but the deep etch of my date of death remained
along with my age of fourteen years.
When a falling ice-laden limb fell and broke off the top of my stone
the bottom was by then anchored in the embrace of my leg
where it still remains, two centuries later,
the tip of gray-black stone protruding above the line of bark
like the tooth of a shark broken off and left
in the flesh of its victim.

I expect the picture in that machine
will be shown to others as remarkable coincidence.
I suppose that is true as I can see the whole graveyard,
now hemmed in by large buildings of brick and stone
ensconced with signs of trade carried out within, and
although there are many trees in my graveyard
there are not many stones remaining,
so many crumbled away
so many carried away
I see no other marker resting in the embrace of a nearby tree,
and thus no soul as blessed as I am
with my eyes upon the world again
and again and again through innumerable seasons.
I hear creaks in my tree these days.
Life being by definition defined by death inevitable,
some day no doubt a wind will come and fell me

bark and branch and needles green;
Then someone with an axe will hack me up for his fire.
My molecules will finally ascend to whatever heaven may
prove to be.
I find a fullness in this, my good fortune.
I find, too, a joy
that a child should see my marker
and understand it is my statement of my eternity,
a promise to be understood, if at all,
by a child who knows not of death.

If you happen to be, some time,
in the town of Newtowne, in the Honorable State of Massachusetts
and find yourself on a byway convenient to the old cemetery
on the hill
at the corner of what was once Needham Great Road and the
path to the River Charles
and if you can trace the modern names to find me
or just stumble on a sparse cemetery on a weedy hill
then please climb the incline to me
the tallest evergreen in sight,
walk around my bark and touch my stone.
I will reciprocate with my blessing from on high and,
my plan be well met,
later with my blessing from higher still.

Until then, Samuel Josephus Carter the Third
bids you adieu,
all my millions of pine needles
wave to you
while my soul rejoices in this Summer sun.

This tree grows out of the grave of a young man born in the year 1810. The trunk of the tree embraces the broken base of his gravestone. The site is on a weedy hillock at a busy intersection surrounded by mundane commercial enterprises. One day in the late Summer of 2020 I found myself waiting for my son to buy wood at the adjacent lumber yard, and climbed the hill to find many stones from the 18th and 19th century, over which towered this huge pine. Walking around its trunk, I found that the tree was itself arising from the melancholy remains of a fourteen year old, taken by unknown cause midst no doubt the greatest of lamentations. The boy and the lamentations are lost to history, leaving this glorious green monument and a sobering lesson for all of us. In this poem, I give him allegorical rebirth, without speculating as to whether his essence gives me thanks.

Hunting the Blues

The sand still exudes the sun
but the warmth dissipates half way up my body.
The wind is fresh
and cold in contrast to the day,
whisking across my face,
carrying a thin spray of salt water.
There is noise, almost cacophony
of waves and rocks pulled and clanged by water,
of hiss of running ocean over fine sand,
of gulls on their diving hunt for small creatures out for
an evening crawl.
Fishing boats, dimly lit fore and aft in red and white light
clouded by fog,
cough towards the docks around the spit,
staccato pounding sound muffled flat of pitch by wetted air.
My half-moon is enough light by which to bait
and not so much to wash away my stars.

The driftwood is set afire, in hopes the lack of permit will not matter.
The folding chair is set just above the receding tide line.
Sunk deep into wet sand are the tubular spikes that hold the rods,
their tips supple and wiggling in the wind.
The ice in the beer cooler has behaved this night;
the plastic package of cigars has been kept dry,
the plastic bag protecting the wind-proof Zippo has not been
breached.

They are out there.
Yes they are.
In the cold scaled flesh of nighttime
with rows of small sharp teeth

and the frantic nightly dance in the moonlight piercing the surface,
a quick swish, a random dart, a clomping bite into what is swept
    offshore by tide
and some small fish has been offered up on Darwin's platter
to transmute to flesh of the mighty blue.
I cast my line, weighted and snelled and hooked with chum
to be carried out by receding waves, mixed with rock and sand and
small sea things and sand things and shrimps and dead crabs
to be culled in rapid sequence, ingested in constant gulps,
razored by teeth in thin line of jaw,
sacrificed to the mighty blue.

My glowing tip will be false a beacon seaward.
The mesh of my chair will let the wind chill me
in my solitary immobile stalking,
my fingers will numb as I reel in my line each ten minutes to see
if something has bitten, if something has been hooked in the bite,
if the ocean has itself swallowed the bits of clam in cheating
    against the blues, or
if some blue of legal size has hooked himself in his seizure
and even now can sense the battle, the pull of heavied line
    through the surf,
flapping on the wet sand, then breaded with dry sand into
    which it flops,
the primal fish feeling primal fear,
of being the eaten, not the eater, and, who knows,
perhaps word has reached back out to the Nantucket Shoals
of the beheading, the scaling, the fileting, the soaking in milky water
to purge the salt and dankness of ocean,
the smoking and the chopping, or the broiling with butter in a pan,
the proxy eating and excretion,

the bones tossed in gritted trash cans already rank with guts—
the loss of body and then of everything.
I have pulled a beauty this night, a thick one, at least 15 pounds
    I wager,
indignant and then frantic for being plucked,
an angry thrashing and jumping, seeking to shed the two hooks
    I see
sunk into a cheek, highlighted with blood and random white flesh.
Does he not know enough to die in his time?
Why must he be so frantic, so resolved, so—human in his rage?
For such moments, good beach fisherman, I extract from my
    plastic garbage bag
a short stock of wood, a billy club for marine use,
a deadly missive brought down sharply on the skull, one two three
thunking times
until the point be made, and all one hears
is, again, the sea.

In the shed I will prepare this fish,
smoke and grind it into bluefish pate,
sell it to Johnny, who has that fancy café down by the harbor.
Johnny will put that ground fish into small glass bowls
at seven dollars for three ounces
(but do not fault him as the crackers must be bought also), and
tourists will dip their rye crackers into my fish,
wash it down with beer,

and think, ‘by God I can almost taste the sea in this’
and think, ‘what else, perhaps the taste of fire in this.’
I will use the eight dollars I am paid for $200 of paté
to buy another cheap cigar,
replacements for the tackle washed to sea, then
take another green trash bag, the coffin of the blues,
walk next clear night with my chair and spike and rod down to
 the littoral,
coax the blues to me, by guile and gear and the beacon of
 tobacco tip
and sit in the cold, feeling blue.

III

NATURE

Spanish Moss

Geese

Cape Cod

Wind and Will

Spring

Summer is Dying

Apples

Ice

Waiting for Snow

Spanish Moss

I have picked up a strand of Spanish Moss,
light and spindly but soft to the touch.
It appears as a crown of thorns, but softened by time
into a lacy memory of things past and gone.
I twirl it around my head as a halo.
I feel like it is sacrilege but it is not.
A soft, fallen, once-living thing
hung as Christmas decoration on a tree,
then freed by gentle wind and nestled on top of green growing grass,
presented to me by the small hands of earth
to hold and marvel and enjoy and bedeck myself.
I cannot see my face but I presume angelic, even holy allusions.
A foursome of sand cranes slowly pick their way towards me,
pecking here and there and looking up at the sky, then at me.
They have landed just a few minutes ago across the field
and have strutted casually forward to inspect me.
They do not caw sharply as is their style.
They approach, they stop pecking, and I can see
in their eyes that they are captivated.
The dark center of each eye is rimmed by orange,
and, beyond that, each a crown of scarlet,
a noble color if not quite purple.
They form a court around me, heads bobbing downwards
and I imagine I feel them praying in recognition.
Peripatetic creatures of serious mien,
they are for this moment at peace.
We stand together in the dappled sun filtering through the trees.
We feel the same feelings, we breathe the same air, and
from the porch,
the wind chimes are announcing we are one.

Geese

There are geese over the city.
They are quite a surprise.
Their necks stretch forward like arrows,
their wings in rhythmic flap,
their formation contradicting their wildness.

I first saw them by the train tracks,
trisected by the overhead wires,
flying segmented gray silhouettes on blue sky,
disappearing behind the tall buildings,
reappearing on cue stage left.

There are not many wild things in the city.
The ducks on the common are permanent and do not count.
There are I suppose the rats and stray cats and sewer snakes
but none of those have majesty invoking the wild.
But geese! From the North, another country!

They are early this year, it is only March.
Proof of a warming world,
harbinger of eternal Springs,
they will fill the river and deface the sidewalks,
accepting no guff from the likes of us.

As all things wild, they will one day leave
as suddenly as they came,
high on the wing, daring to dream.
So while they are here we must pay attention:
there is nothing so sad as a wonder that is ignored.

Cape Cod

Black blobs bouncing on gray-green water
out there
many yards from shore.
The tide surrenders in white foaming protest
onto the beach
sating sun-parched sand.
Children point, whistles blow.
Parents drag whining reticent bodies
inland, trailing feet behind.
It is hard to surrender past patterns,
memories of sand in sandwiches
and banging into surf on passing whim.
There is a new flag waving off the guard stand,
not green for safety,
not red for rip tide,
there is black for blood
flapping and snapping in the winds of fright
of that beyond the beaches, unimaginable.
My son squirms, baking
on our stained blanket,
looking up-beach for the ice cream truck.
We cannot toss our ball
as the shoreline is jammed full with the likes of us
hiding, cluttering the strand
while, near enough to hear
if sound were water-soluble,
slipping in dark coolness
it slides and squiggles and dreams
of fat and flesh
and reassuring overtones of ocean.

Black bobbers on the top
float innocently
awaiting choice
as it shops the shelves of the sea
for its favored brand
today and forever.
Looking to sea
we imagine inevitable horrors
though there is no evil, only what is true.
And when one black bobber
out beyond the breaker line
is deleted from view
I turn and rub lotion on my son's back,
a trace of sand mixed in for texture though by accident
and explain to him the flag.
He is as unimpressed as was the seal
whose flesh now hangs in shards from pointed teeth
out beyond the breakers.
Children and seals
see end of life abstract and impersonal,
contemplating the lacy edge of the sea as it leaves bubbles on
 the littoral.
Staring seaward, I see death biting into the heart of the world.

Wind and Will

The wind is from the ocean. From the South-West.
It is the prevailing wind although
I have never been told against whom it has been victorious.
The flags are snapping and dancing.
The smoke is horizontal to the ground as soon as it exits its chimney.
People are hunched and hurried, harried by flapping scarfs,
closed around themselves as if it were not so warm,
defensed against the expectation that the wind is, as is often said, "ill."

The wind itself has confided to me that it is indifferent to its impact on people.
A free agent, it blows for its own account, with a will of its own.
If its strings are pulled by others,
by weather or sun or sea or spin
it is not sharing that information with the likes of me.
You may have better luck if you choose to inquire.
We have never been close,
the wind and I.

I have had, it is true, passing acquaintance,
good times even,
with its children, the breezes, but children always are more
accessible,
less defensive than their parents,
so I do not consider myself a true friend.
But I am familiar and do not fear.
I enjoy the hearty blow, the arctic blast, the insistent off-shore,
the hard-charging Nor'easter
although I confess disapproval of twisters, which are just a
matter of showing off.

There is no such thing as a wind that's ill,
it's just a wind that has free will.
We might do well to emulate and
rather than cower, just celebrate.

Spring

Thus are the epiphanies of Spring:
Rivulets flowing,
cold water over stones still set in ice
clear with floating sparkles.
Ponds edged in frost
clasp leaves of last Fall and browned reeds
sheltering small schools of darting fish
making waves before my shadow.
Dark bush brambles tipped with green
suggest blooms but for now
hold their silence.
Woodpeckers tap,
hidden flies reborn to buzz,
hidden birds of indistinct lineage
whose calls you promised yourself to learn
last year but failed.
Flowers at path's edge
where glints of sun weave through tree branches
and warm the margins while
in the fields
green grass explodes in random pattern
amid snow shrunken to patchwork.
Ducks on river:
did they ever really go home, South you presume,
and so quickly return, or
did they hide in the shrouds of Winter
to be available now to surprise?
No matter. They are bobbing and paddling to no
visible purpose.

Deep beneath birches, wings of white bark flap in the wind,
sentinels over absurd orange mushrooms
scattered abruptly about by an unseen magician
as an act of magic.
Deeper still, the pines protect the cones beneath
    unyielding snow
but as I walk there is crunch of needles that almost rustle
beneath my boots.

We learn by rumor
children then
that Spring is rebirth and thus happy.
No doubt the color and the sound can attract
quickening of heart.
We ignore the vast sacrifice of growth and death
which sets the stage for what we call Spring.

I have yet to see the inevitable robin
hopping red and openly over blotches of shining snow melt,
harbinger of warmth and mirth,
so I cannot declare Spring official quite yet.

When I do, I shall open my cellar,
haul up half-rusted chairs and tables,
molded umbrella,
chair cushions of striped green,
summer dishes,
go to the store and order what corporeal things are needed,
along with sprightly white wines

to invite friends and those we would impress to come
sit and sip my wine, feel the sun,
speculate on the weather and the earliness of the season
scan the hedgerow for the hint of small birds
ogle the tree line to see and mark for the hunt the dappled fawn
and acquiesce at last in declaring the arrival of a Spring.
Then, thus encouraged, I shall write another poem about Spring—
No not this one but an official declaration
published in some well-regarded journal of modest circulation
So that friends will come to share glasses of Prosecco
and tell me they enjoyed my most recent published piece.

Across the field my old dog vainly chases a dauntless cottontail
which thinks it can afford to drift from side to side and still not
be caught.
Its white-tail is a trope of Spring, sometimes dropped bloodied
at my door by a smiling dog
who does not eat rabbit after all but intuits his role to kill and offer.
His ritual of Spring.

We are
or may be
so different, my dog and I
as each of us weaves down the path in the sun
of our shared afternoon.

Summer is Dying

The rattle of continually falling acorns occupies my porch,
their sharp pings make me awaken with a start.
Heralds of cold they are,
a fact you have repressed all of August.
But your calendar trumpets September,
the month that turns upon the year with bared teeth,
baiting us with a warm day or two and then,
we outside in thin garb because we can see there is sunshine,
it invades our armholes, our sockless feet casually ensconced
  in our loafers,
our unprotected necks,
our chests needing one more layer,
fading our perfected tans,
compelling us to school or its unfortunate handmaiden of
  employment,
depressing our spirits in cruel reversal
until we sour on ourselves,
a depression neither bee-attended cider nor over-fat dirty
  pumpkins can dispel.

Today I glanced outside at what I was sure was September's
  last viable seduction,
a day so clear and yet moist that it sucked at my pores, pulling
  outward.
I am a paper man, a computer man, a phone man, a deal man,
  a family man, a modern man,
a mature man whom no one would dare, today, call "dude."
So there is no excuse, even though my offer to flee was rejected
  with suspicious smiles by all I approached.

Well, one can be one's best self alone and, perhaps, only alone.
The paper computer phone deal family modern mature man can be found,
open air café down the street with a view of the harbor,
alone at his table,
a bottle of Sancerre and an iced glass,
a plate of soft cheese and toast points,
sunglasses down,
legs crossed,
smiling at September
because I have called its bluff, I know its game, I am high on
the crested wave that will not fall if I do not look downward.

Apples

Dew makes slick the shining skin
as I twist don't pull
and feel at last the quiet snap
that puts the apple in my hand,
my mouth—
it's so grand
so sweet
I eat them all,
standing there midst row on row of drooping trees,
their branches grazing the buzzing earth
with squishing squashing stepped upon falling fallen
green and yellow and red and speckled
and wormy bird pecked simply dropped apples,
would be ciders soft and hard,
pies sweet and tart
the mother of all good things of Fall
now underfoot and humming with flies and bees,
snacking on sugar and yellowing meat.
We taste of each as we make our way,
bag bursting, dropping newest treasures to the ground.
Which ones are for cooking, which for sauce, which to eat?

Spread on the hillside is the orchard
in the heart of Massachusetts
to which each September we find our way,
to drink cider with hot donuts small and sugared,
and harvest apples, carrying still the wounds of original sin:
Oh Cortlands, Oh Macs, oh odd-named Macouns
Oh green Granny Smiths
Oh greener Green Crispins all the way from Japan,
Yes Braeburns, yes Galas in wild celebration,
Delicious Delicious both dark red and golden as butter!

My stomach screams “stop” but the mind overpowers
and, crunching and sucking while homeward driving,
the perfume of apples fills both lungs and nostrils.

Back home, trouser bottoms soaked wet and still clinging
to stockings and shins with small leaves still hanging,
we pile up our apples, forgetting their species,
and declare that the Fall is our most favored season.

Ice

At last the ice has come.
At last, at last!
My pond is capped by sheens of glitter.
The late fall sun, diffused and fuzzed
through early morning haze
shoots pure white light skittering over the glaze,
an expanding highway of light sliding over cold wetness
and running up upon the shore, where
it weaves its way over leaves, among trees,
past browning brittle droppings,
warms my face, diffused by distance,
through the craggy maple's few hangers-on,
watching the elm leaves going to yellow,
prisms of color woven into the flow.

The ducks are gone.
They no longer drift in shallow corners
where they show their rumps all Summer,
sucking unseen things from the imagined bottom,
sluggy slimey morsels left undefined.
Custom has them flying South
but I never knew them to fly.
I see them rather cozied in some nearby barn,
or hunkered beneath some aging car in a near-collapsing garage,
swinging door half opened on rusted hinges,
or in some near-by running river warmed by run-off from the
fields, or
heated by distant kiln or furnace,
waiting out the ice,
uninformed that their wait will be too long.

I descend to the embankment edge,
brushing past low limbs and naked bush,
and gently toe the surface of the pond.
My mind informs me not to step,
it is too early in the season;
the fractured lines extending from my foot
give further witness to November.
I must await the dark mornings of deep winter
before I walk carefully over the thickened ice,
later still before I strap on skates and let the heavy weight
concentrate into the sharpened blades,
gently sliding with certain balance,
the message of the ice rising through my boots into my core.
Then I will follow the road of white light to the Eastern shore
and gaze fully into its muted source,
reaching out with invisible tendrils for the warm birth of it.

Today, the ice is thin as a robin's eggshell,
echoing its pale countenance in subtle calling.
My waiting will of course presage Spring, the death-knell of ice
and with the melt the Spring will call to darning needles
    flickering the surface,
wake the ducks from their slumber,
mirror the pale green that promises the warmth of Summer.
But for now I am looking only to December, to January,
    to February before a thaw.
Perhaps also I will cut a hole in the surface,
sit on a folding chair,
drop a line into the chill water of the pond
waiting contentedly although, of course,
no fish larger than a sunny has ever graced its shallowness.

I have a broom to clear unwanted snow.
The ice is what declares the heralding of cold.
When the snow presumes to pile itself too deep to brush away
I will dig one small patch to stand upon
as I am a man for ice, truth be told.
Underneath I sense the rush of chill water,
yearning vainly for the touch of white light.
How that water must envy me then.
The water awaits that day when, coat open to warming air
I stand at the edge and dare not step again.
Well, we all of us dream, in our way.

Waiting for Snow

I have been sitting at my kitchen table
impatiently waiting for the promised snow.
It has been cold all day, with the flat gray sky
and chilled wind
that often herald deep snow.
People tell me that it is coming our way.
It is warm in here,
but I chill often as I open the door to my porch,
then close it in disappointment of seeing the unconcealed woods.
I turn my palm upwards in vain search for cold droppings,
even random flakes would satisfy.
It is night now and I fear I will miss the falling,
only awakening when the falling is over,
so all that is left to me is the shovel and the ice
with nostrils frozen shut in my effort.
I am too old to shovel snow, I am told,
but we have an agreement, snow and I.
It falls and I move it into convenient places,
so that both of us are happy.
I can look at its whiteness,
sense its coldness,
admire its pureness.
It can strut its karma,
appreciating the paths I have made for its admirers to approach.

I have gotten up,
taken a sip of my coffee,
gone to the front door
where there are brighter lights and
indeed something is falling,
a thin mist that has coated my lawn and walkway.

But this is not the snow I welcome,
this frozen drizzle that coats the ground.
It is dull and incessant, chilly and impudent, and
worse yet,
it will coat the world with ice
so when we walk through the snow that will come, I am sure,
we will slip on the slick underside,
slide and strain and fall and curse
and people will tell us we deserved what we got when we limp home.
I will sit now, by my front window,
front lights glaring into the night,
waiting for the coming of huge flakes,
drifting in demure descent,
mocking this faux snow now drizzling down.
I will open the door and stand on my steps
and enjoy the cold of gently dropping water doilies
as they spend a moment on my tongue
before gladly becoming part of me.
You will not find any lines of poetry here
about that moment, nor about the times after
as I diffuse into the whiteness.
I will be busy with the snow,
and not have time to tell you about it.

IV

I/ID

Mary

I Want You (Now)

Can't Win

Road Trip

Burnt Chocolate

No Refund

Seasons

Cold

I Am at Sea

I Am as Mercury

Outer Space

I Am Walking Down the Street

Lickety-Split

More

And Dreams Were Made and Used and Wasted

The Disappearing Dream

Pick-Up Lines

Whom Do I Want to Be Today?

Mary

There was a wound
walking down the street
escaping the body to which it belonged
as if the pain could be excised
exported
exhumed
by force of will
dripping blood on the street.

And here I was,
my blood far away in drips drabs drops
and no way to mend the breach unless
the pain could leave and the wound remain
to be salved
saved
sutured
by force of will
in the corners of my mind.

Mary dropped the knife
on her way out the window
to remind me that the wound
was separate from myself
herself
all selves
by force of will
removed for all time.

I declare I wish to be whole.
I wish to carry my pain
my wound
my blood
my cure
my salvation
the remains of my will
when the timepiece chimes.

I do not know what I miss most:
Mary or the knife.

I Want You (Now)

I was coy for a while.
  How about you?

I was crazed by desire from the start.
  How about you?

I will no longer be still.
  How about you?

Do I proceed by guile?
  How about you?

I am not to be denied.
  How about you?

I will be satisfied.
  I will not ask you.

Can’t Win

She said she was feeling off center that day,
I asked if centered was her favorite way.
I was told that was not the point.

She was feeling, another time, good but alone,
I said she was resting in her own body’s home.
I was told that was not a sensitive thing to say.

She once felt elated with power and joy,
I joined her excitement so as not to annoy.
I was told I was stealing her moment.

She was finally angry and said she would leave.
I begged her to stay, her departure would grieve.
I was told that to beg her was selfish.

She is finally gone, our house is now still.
I can say what I want and do what I will.
I tell myself that is fine.

And nobody told me anything different.

Road Trip

You offered me solace, but
I explained I was of the practice of seeking comfort
in my own way.
Looking in the mirror,
this time,
I sensed things askew,
pieces missing, or perhaps just misplaced.
Lacking energy to search or rearrange,
I looked away.
Since then I have enjoyed making condolence calls
at homes of friends who have suffered a death.
I find comfort in the mirrors draped in black cloth,
no image staring back.

In a poker game, back room of a bar open after hours,
in a town I was passing through,
driving West,
I found myself winning constantly at small stakes,
so much so I was being looked at with suspicion.
A taciturn man gave out a sense of menace.
Fearing consequences, I began to throw away better hands
but then, it was suggested that the stakes be doubled.
I felt compelled to play until I had lost all my winnings
and then some, before I felt safe letting out a yawn,
announcing I must be on my way.
Life is risk that bites you
on the downside when the stakes are high.
Everyone's pile grew but mine
with no one to blame but myself.

I have taken to sleeping in my car
which seems more secure.
The seats recline almost all the way
and the lumps contour to my body.
The smell is familiar and unsullied
so that I feel self-contained.
Most times I can sleep in parking lots of large malls,
although on occasion I am asked by security to move on.

In Las Vegas, the police are vigilant all through the night,
no doubt a reflection of the pace and restlessness.
I was arrested there for vagrancy when I could not produce a
hotel key
but released the next morning when the magistrate was handed
my wallet
by the jailer.
"Why you sleeping in your car, you've got credit cards and
hundreds of dollars?"
I said I felt tired and needed to rest from driving West.
He shook his head and returned to his paperwork.

In California the ocean was cold and the wind was brisk.
I took my tent and walked a mile or so down a pebbled beach,
slept undisturbed for a few days
but ran out of chips and beer and moved on.

I have been here before, I thought each day
as I found myself elsewhere
in places I had never been.
You are your own place, you carry it with you,
and that's the truth.

I am headed back home soon.
I will thank my cousin for watching the place
these many months
unless he has trashed it
as is his history.
Some people make a mess of where they stay.
Others make a mess of where they go.

Burnt Chocolate

I melted into day and stood on the corner
with flowers at my feet and in my hair.
I was the essence on the wind although the wind simply was not pleased.
Below me in the world there was strife and candy canes and a hint of pestilence
and suddenly it was night.
If I am floral
am I in a vase or in your nostrils?
If I am iron am I in the ground or holding up your apartment house?
If I am flesh—
well, no, that is too unlikely and I have nothing to say about that.
The day waned and I waned and we were both gone and the flowered iron of the night
spoke to me of incompatible destinies
while chocolate bubbled in the pot and burned.

No Refund

I have a disquieting ennui.
You are anti-social.
I am irritated by major events.
You are allergic to all of life.
I am forthcoming in matters of the heart.
You are closed.
I play well with others.
You play with others.
I am raising my child with concern for the outcome.
You are raising your child with an outcome of concern.
People stand when I enter a room.
People cannot stand it when you enter a room.
I think sex is wonderful.
You think sex is war.
I think love is encompassing.
You don't think of love as anything.
All I have
is this disquieting ennui.

Seasons

It was Summer one day when I last held you
as the various heats of day and body mixed,
an inseparable concert
while sheets twisted and trapped our legs in chains.

It is poetic to blame the Winter for future chill
but the calendar is happenstance,
silent observer to the pace of love and not love,
where touch becomes revulsion
and each smile is misunderstood.

You were all I wished you to be
but in my desires, I was mistaken.
Desires follow neither seasons nor logic.
Lust follows eons of hidden imperative.

I helped you pack your luggage
and watched your footsteps mark passage in the snow.
I have only myself to blame, I know, but
now that you are gone
I choose to blame it all on you.

And on Winter.

Cold

It is cold, we are told;
arctic invasion, source unclear.
Out for a walk, colder than the South Pole they say
here in the City.

Makes you think
  I think
about how cold you have been,
how cold things are,
and what is the signature of cold.

Is it as cold as the heart of a woman scorned.
Cold as the heart of the cuckolded man with Italian horns
on a chain.
Cold as the mind of the physicist at his desk
splitting atoms in his head to make a bomb.
Cold as the day you left me.
Cold as the day you returned, and why.
Cold as I see you in your robe half opened as a threat.

What is the temperature of your touch and how to calibrate?
What is the climate of your soul and how to equivocate?
What is the wind chill of your chill and why is there wind at all
in the frozen chambers of the evening when the cold bodies
effervesce into crystal?
And why is it not dark? Are not cold and dark the handmaidens
of the fiction that vainly tries to define the meaning of cold?
Perhaps that is why the fiction fails.

I have captured cold in my eye with the sight of death, and of
rheumatics and of failure and of envy and of you.
I have captured cold in my heart with the feeling of desertion
and of rhymes and of anger and of emptiness and of you.
I have captured cold in my ears with the sound of saws cutting
concrete and with breath of hard dust and of rhythms and of
solicitude and of you.
I have captured cold in my mouth with ice of frozen acids and
splinters of shards of strips of slices of vile rot and of you.

It is cold, we are told,
as if to go outdoors is a risk to us, a frostbite of the body,
a clogged nostril, a pneumonia of the flesh.
I was outside today. That is not cold.
There is light and fire in the world, people and things
whirr and function.

The weatherman would come to you
if he only knew
he then could calibrate the end of things
by the single point of you
where all motion stops
and atoms go to die.

I Am at Sea

I am sailing hardened up and gunwales down.
The sea foams past me as I lean back against the force of the wind.
I am going as fast as I dare which is as fast as I can but
I am confused.

It is all about the sail as there is no seen destination,
  just bobbing horizon.
I recall a lighthouse now and again but the fog obscures my view.
My compass has taken on water, an unfortunate development
and I am feeling lost.

Now the water is afloat with colored flowers
and with corpses of people I know.
Now the water is afloat with tombstones
Borne by porpoises whose eyes seem closed.

My children float past, their own boats with reefed sails.
They are going nowhere, while I, at least, am headed somewhere.
Their boats are without compass. I had our compass
but it failed us all.

Wind from the North brings glints of sun,
from the South the rising of the moon,
from the East the birth of all things
and from the West I am sailing the prevailing wind.

Women sit forward, hair stringy with brine
shot through with gray hairs and dead memories.
Perhaps it is only the memories I am seeing.
How is one to know?

The tiller is cold and slick, my grip tight but cramping.
If I lose the stick, what then? Do I come up still in the water?
My boat in irons?
My heart rusts in salt and beats nonetheless.

I pray to hit a beach, full tilt is fine, I need to stop.
I will roll off the deck and crawl up the sand and lie face down
  in salvation.
The ocean is time, the wind is my life, my sail is spilling wind
as the rose petals float my highway across the waves.

I am as Mercury

I am as Mercury,
so small as to be missed by all but most discerning observers,
circling a world so bright that my subtle (imagined) attributes
are not obvious to the casual glance, or
sometimes
often
orbiting below the plane of vision,
obscured even by the lowest of hills and
indeed
even by shrubs or blades of grass.
I circle quickly in search of meaning
only to return each few days to the very same place in heaven
from which I started.

Why do I bother, did you ask?
It is all I know.
It is warm
and it does not change itself upon me,
requiring me to change, a bothersome thing.

Do I ever think I would like to break free, you inquired?
To what end?
I would spin wildly into the dark unknown regions of time,
anticipating the excitement of something new, but
new things are often not good things, you know,
and it is cold out there.
And dark.

I am even now feeling the pull of my reality as my wild escape
slows,
halts at apogee,
then draws me down again in ever-increasing streaks
by inexorable unseen ill-understood forces
racing past saucy Venus, presumptuous tart lit up for all to see
until I am, disquieted, disheartened, disappointed and
debilitated,
where I began it all,
where you first suggested I dare and I succumbed for once
to the caprice of something better.

I am Mercury ruled by my sun,
heated by its power,
devoid of life and air and flowers and oceans it is true
(stripped away eons ago by my voracious master and now a
naked pink thing in the sky)
but nonetheless content to know my path.

If you cannot see me, you cannot judge me.

Outer Space

I am tendrils of fire.
Protruding burning flesh.
Core of a star.
Penumbras of pain.

I am aimed at you.
Intervening bodies bend my passion
and warp my light.
They fail fully to intercede.

My rays parch your fields.
My emanations tick the body atomic.
Your flesh shreds to eddies.
I am master of all that remains.

I once had compassion
but now there is no use.
I destroy it to own it.
I am defined in how you must cower.

We are ascendant.
You are descendant.
The top of your head remains for a moment
and then, you are gone.

Cold space has no memory
of things that used to be.
Dark matter passes through it
with no regard for me.

I Am Walking Down the Street

I am walking down the street
in the Fall of 1957 and it is darkening and chill.
My head is down to deflect the wind.
The brownstone houses are fading to gray
as the sun sets over Brooklyn.
The smell of boiled cabbage leaks into the growing evening.
"Excuse me, yes, you young man. You're Jewish, yes?"
I want to deny it.
The temerity of the question!
And to what end could it be asked?
But we are raised,
we Jews of America, in this place and time
with the death camps strapped to our backs.
We are compelled to be fierce,
as fierce as we can muster,
in admitting, defending, brandishing our Jewness,
lest we cause others to think us weak,
lest they do it to us again in our lifetimes.
Oh, we know they will do it again,
"it" is engrained in the history of all things.
But, Yahweh willing, not on my watch.

"Yes, yes," I reply, diffident yet eager,
keeping my voice calm.
It is a fact not to be denied, hidden or glorified.
"You will please come with me,"
the man asks, but it is a statement and not a question.
I follow him a few doors down, past brownstone stoops.
He is short and shaped like a pear.
He rocks to each side as he walks.

He is of some middle age I cannot understand.
His skull cap is embroidered in bright colors.
His beard is so dark and full that
from the rear
its sides stick out beyond his head
and create a picture frame.
From the edges of his dark jacket
white ritual fringes flutter with each step.

In the front parlor are now ten Jews,
nine men and me.
I am given a skull cap and a prayer book.
There are now enough Jews for the afternoon prayers.
They are needed, any ten,
we are all the same before Elohim,
fungible witnesses to five thousand years of suffering,
rocking back and forth and praying
in this guttural foreign tongue.
Reciting prayers I do not precisely understand,
cannot translate.
I struggle to read the Hebrew words,
embarrassed in the presence of these adults
that I am so unlearned.
But they do not care.
They understand.
They know that there are Jews and then there are Jews.
Some can daven, can pray in dissonant cadence,
their eyes shut tight in pious submission.
Some cannot.
Some are not believers in Yahweh.
Others are not sure:
So many burned women and children,

cousins and aunts still mourned that they never left the old country
until they could no longer leave on boats
and then they left as smoke.
So it is enough to these men I do not know
that I am standing there, mumbling an occasional prayer
  I can recall.
I am, too, a witness, to
the unwilling but inevitable future of whatever it will bring
upon my people,
upon me,
upon my children.

The air is rich with cheap cologne and garlic,
the room is dark and almost empty,
and we rock and chant together, each in his own way.
We are chanting beside the Red Sea,
we are chanting high on Masada,
we are chanting before the Wall,
we are chanting in York as we are expelled,
we are chanting as we are boiled in Spanish oil,
we are chanting at the gates of Dachau,
we are chanting on the street where last Tuesday I was called
a goddamned kike.

And then we are done chanting.
I hand back my skull cap and prayer book,
wordlessly.

An old man takes them, looks up at my face
with a thin smile
and, holding his handkerchief,
wipes the tears from my cheeks.

Lickety-Split

Lickety-split, lickety-split,
sliding down the edge of tomorrow.
Don't like this feeling one damn bit,
feels like the promise of sorrow.

Ever find yourself in a very bad place
even though you're living straight arrow?
Ever feel low when they throw it in your face
while you're trying for the clean and narrow?

They always tell you that life's like that,
so do your best to do good.
Don't dirty yourself doing tit for tat,
just always behave like you should.

As for me, I'm feeling fine,
no moss on this rolling stone.
Do the job and toe the line.
Work yourself down to the bone.

Somehow, though, darkness follows me,
evil sneaks into my head.
Not the way that I want to be,
but see, it's just like I said:

Sooner or later, you can go astray,
drooling in another man's beer,
and you pay the price that very day
and afterwards live with your fear.
I still keep trying to do my bit,
and never beg, steal or borrow,
but lickety-split, lickety-split,
I'm sliding down the edge of tomorrow.

More

I gain by labor.
(I steal.)
I gain by force.
(I steal.)
I gain by inheritance.
(They stole.)
I gain by cabal.
(We steal.)
I gain by my gods.
(Their acolytes steal.)
I gain by your fears.
(My comforting steals.)
I gain by your love.
(I steal from you.)

And Dreams Were Made and Used and Wasted

When do dreams go stale, I wonder?

It used to be
before some point in time and space that I do not recall
that I dreamed of future things:
women, excitement, beaches.
After that
(when was that, anyway?)
and all of a sudden,
it was all about memories.
Is it really a dream if it already happened?

I am not talking about those bad dreams,
those cold sweat dreams when you sit up in bed and say to yourself,
"What the hell was that?"

I am not talking about those dreams, even worse, that do not fade
so you wake up disquieted but not fully awake and,
against your will, drift back to sleep and into that dream,
knowing you are falling falling . . .

I am talking about the dreams of daylight,
sitting on your porch with your eyes closed
as the first warmth of Spring dares you to dream.

I am talking about the dreams you have
when you tell yourself, "I am in a great place,
so why don't I let myself loose and dream a dream."

I am dreaming now that I am writing a poem about my dreams
and they are not dreams.
I am living now and I am writing a poem about my dreams
and they are not dreams.
I am sitting now, wondering where all those dreams go when
they are dreamed out
in the lost-sock drawer of my mind.

The Disappearing Dream

As a child, how old I do not recall,
I had a dream that a man in black was chasing me with a beaker
containing a liquid that made you disappear.
I was running, running, for many many nights running
but I was tired, and a child, and he was gaining on me and then
he was close enough to toss and slosh the liquid towards me,
he could not catch me, as somehow he just could not but
over time
he was able to splash me, a drop here
another drop there and
wherever the drop fell, my clothes and body disappeared,
neat round holes in me.
The liquid of course fell ground-ward and soon
my feet and legs were gone but I still moved forward somehow
and I was so tired, so many nights, so many terrors that
one night I said to myself, just stop running
and let him put an end to you
and I surrendered at last and paused but did not turn
until I was drenched in liquid
awake in a sea of sweat and urine.
My mother yelled that I was too old for that
(I never dreamed that dream again . . .).

Pick-up Lines

There are not many things I would pick up off the street.
Not many things of value are there for the taking.
As a child, I would bend for a penny.
Today, I would not.
As a youngster, I found a ten dollar bill
(back when a dollar was a dollar, as my dad used to say);
when I clutched it in my hand
and ran to my mother:
"Look, mom, I found a ten dollar bill!"
She said in a soft voice
"Well, quick put it in your pocket or some stranger will come,
smile and say, 'excuse me but did you folks happen to see
a ten dollar bill on the ground
because I think I dropped it when I reached for my
pack of cigarettes.' "

I will pick up a quarter. I will pretend not to see a dime.
I will pick up a lottery ticket. You never know.
I will pick up a wallet of course
or anything that shines like gold.
I pick up keys and put them hopefully on the nearest flat surface.
Same with one glove, or a hat. Unless they are soaked.

I will pick up a parking receipt for a car that is unclaimed, but
when you think about it, there is not much to do with it.
I stop to look at face-up business cards; I will turn my head or
move around them so I can read them.
But I will not pick them up.

You seldom see a photograph on the street.
These days you seldom see any photographs at all, except on a telephone screen.
A photograph is almost an abandoned antique.
I always want to pick them up, but they seem too personal.
So often I leave them on the ground.

In the City I have picked up
money, lottery tickets, wallets, credit cards,
pictures of women,
a watch that had no insides,
a ring that turned out to be bait for a nearby scam artist,
keys, gloves, one hat,
one Swiss Army Knife,
a pocket Swedish-English dictionary,
reading glasses,
an earring with small diamonds
and an unused bus ticket to Nashua, New Hampshire.
I have saved these things
in a Muriel's Air-Tip cigar box that I took from a neighbor's trash.
It is under my bed.
I keep the cover closed.

Whom Do I Want to Be Today?

Did you ever dream who you would be
if you could be anybody?

Not a specific person, those jobs are taken.

Just the person being you,
filling some role,
then basking in some direct or reflected glory,
giving yourself the glow that is missing from your life.

At my desk, over coffee, I imagined a list of today's new role for me:

I am sitting at a window table in a café, drizzle in the city street, in a woman's coat, fur collar, holding a copy of Elizabeth Barrett Browning's poetry, one long-stemmed rose between the pages, bloom showing out. "Banal," says a voice. "Perhaps, but it is so beautiful," I reply.

I am a body double in Hollywood; my recent jump off the fourth floor into a swimming pool caught the camera, and the eye of the famous star who has taken off her shirt, revealing sharp tan lines.

Washington turns to me and asks if the timing is right to cross the river; the fires of Trenton shimmer across the flat half-frozen surface of the water.

Leonard Bernstein shakes my hand; I hastily transfer my bow into my left palm being careful not to scratch my violin.

The Martian ice cap crunches beneath my boot; I cannot hear the sound.

My Seventh Grade French teacher is twelve, holding the barbed wire. I cut the wire in the nighttime, and she places her hand in mine and steps into the darkness. The blue numbers on her forearm can no longer be seen.

Willie Nelson leans toward me and tells me it's been a pleasure to be on the same stage with me. The whiskey on his breath is strong but I do not turn away.

God asks how she is doing. I struggle to answer, as the examination is graded "pass/fail."

My mother tells me again that she loves me. The dirt has not penetrated her pine box.

V

GOD AND FAMILY

Barley

I am surrounded by strange things:
bags of barley,
blue jeans of various sizes,
plaid wool shirts,
children's sandals
and a pile of heavy work boots.

The living room is small, antique.
Furniture of a type often on sidewalks awaiting the junk truck.
One torch lamp with frazzled beige shade.
Coffee table chipped at the edges,
red leather top mottled with rings from undrunk tea cups.

The three barrels fill most of the room.
We are interspersed: my parents, my stooped aunt Crainie, my older uncle Yussel.
They are speaking Yiddish.
I am listening, uncomfortable with this proof of non-assimilation.

First, pour in a base of grain for stability,
quarter-filling the 55 gallon drums.
Add a layer of blue jeans,
then more barley,
some children's shoes,
more grain and clothing like a seven layer cake and
finally, on top we spread work boots and a sprinkle of barley.

We are silent.
Dust from the barley defines thin slats of sun cutting into the room.

My father hammers the tops of each barrel.
We apply the labels, several sets.
My father has written the English, my uncle the Russian.

The trucks: Ginsberg Express,
friends of my father.
Two wiry men, strong of arm,
lift the barrels and wrestle them down worn marble stairs
and drive off into the early afternoon.

There are relatives I do not know.
Cousins of many times removed.
They have stared out at me from unfocused photographs.
There are farm animals dimly arrayed behind them.
East of Germany, many kilometers from Leningrad,
lost in poverty and dimness,
I am told they await our barrels.

There are letters, which come slowly.
"The weather has been sunny" means the barrels have arrived
bearing needed wares albeit stripped at the border of the work boots.
"I have not been feeling well" means they have not received
    the barrels or
sometimes
they have arrived with nothing but barley
topped by a layer of human excrement.

It is a fall Sunday in Brooklyn, 1949;
my seventh year.
Barley dust coats the furniture of the living room.
We sit, breathing heavily,
sneezing into the face of the world.

Grandma's Skin

My grandmother was very old.
She appeared in local newspapers, a featured article about
being very old.
She took in a boarder when 103.
"He's an old man," she explained.
Which reply almost exhausted her English.
Her Russian was incomprehensible even to native Russians.
Her Yiddish was passable, but
conversations tended to be one-sided:
she was quite deaf.

Grandma referred to our wives as "the wife"
and to our husbands as "the man."
She baked strudel for relatives in distant cities,
then handed the Irish mailman the hot baking and said
"This is for my brother Yussel in Ohio."
The postman would call my aunt then,
they would meet at the post office
and together wrap and mail the strudels at end of day
which is what you do when someone is very old.

On her hundredth birthday she prepared for her party
by mowing her sloping lawn with a hand-reel Sears mower.

People wanted her recipes.
She would invite them to the kitchen
to watch.
They would gently stop her hand in mid-air
in an effort to measure the quantity of spice or herbs she was
about to drop in;
pinch-full or palm-full or hand-full or a bunch or maybe more.

Her favorite English phrase was: "God bless the Social Security."

Long ago, in the then-farmlands West of Boston
she raised five children.
When the barn burned down, horse and cat and all,
she then sat beside her husband,
working her foot-treadle Singer sewing machine,
piecework garments,
each piece was sewn for a blessing.

She seldom spoke of Russia but
when she did
she would spit,
same as she did whenever she was putting a new shirt on me:
you spit out the evil spirit.

When my grandfather died she did not cry.

She was born when Franklin Pierce was President and
  Nicholas the First was Tsar.
Neither made good omens.
Pierce died from alcohol on his New Hampshire farm
and Nicholas, neurotic tyrant tutored by a Scotswoman,
married for politics to a German princess,
scourge of his people,
giant in bearing and in evil
taken by pneumonia just after her birth and,
one may hope as a result of it.

Today I looked down on my hands.
Veins show through the backs, too close to the surface.

Brown patches float on top.
Lines furrow my wrist.
My grandmother would entertain us by showing us the back
of her hand,
pinching a bit of it and watching as it peaked between her fingers,
but when she released her hold the skin just stayed there,
a small mountain of static flesh.
She would then pinch our hands
and we would stare as our flesh, released,
fell smartly back down to join the flat surface.

I reach down and tentatively pinch my skin
and fearfully release it.
It falls back flat, but
—am I imagining this or not?—
it is falling slowly, slower than in the past,
surely slower than when, as a child,
I sat next to my grandmother, smelling the soap on her skin.

Stones

There is a plastic cup on an end-table in my den, filled with
small stones.
The size of stones where perhaps a dozen would fill your palm.
They are gray and ordinary and without artistic merit.
They are not like the striated stones of black and gray and white
which sit is a crystal bowl in my office,
immersed in clear water so that they gleam as when I found them.
These stones are for graves.
When you visit your parents, or at least the growing grass now
proxy for them,
you are to place a small stone on top of their tombstones.
It is a record of love and remembrance, they say.
It is the Jewish way.
I remember them well,
sometimes with love and sometimes with guilt.
Their tombstones call me, bereft of sufficient small stones.
I imagine they are saddened, embarrassed before all the other
buried Jews
that their only son does not often visit,
and I wonder if they know that, there being no rocks left
on the ground,
I have on rare visits wordlessly taken stones from other graves
and placed them in honor of my parents.
This graveyard is of the newest style, their names are on flush
metal plaques embedded primly in the earth,
not really tombstones at all although that is what we call them.
All you can do is drop the stones on the plaques until they tumble
over the margins and disappear into the grass.
So the others who have departed us have piles of little rocks and
no paucity of remembrance; they cannot really miss what I steal
for good purpose.

I do not visit often for good reason.
In the cold weather it is cold.
In the warm weather there are things to do.
The graveyard is far away, in an unattractive part of another suburb.
It does them no good, my visits.
They are not coming back to this life and
I do not believe I will see them in another.

When I do visit my wife cries; she loved them,
but I do not cry even though I loved them.
Well sometimes I cry, but not very much.
And am I crying for them, or for me?
My youngest son looks around with discomfort;
his acquaintance with death is marginal.
He is processing the future and thankful it is far away.
But next time I will bring my own small stones.

I have picked them up in sundry places, paths, promenades,
by-ways of chance when, glancing down, I think of my parents
and pick up a stone and bring it home and drop it in the cup.
For someday.
The very act of remembrance, picking up the stone and carrying
   it home,
ought to be enough.

Dresden Woman

Would you like my mother's Dresden woman with harp?
It was an antique when my mother bought it in the 1950s.
When she aged, she started giving away her favorite things,
fearful they would fall into disrepair or alien hands on her demise.
She sought for her things a known afterlife
which was to be denied to her own self.

My mother grew old in a bad, forgetful way.
She would go back to her kitchen,
when planning to leave her house,
to check that the stove burners were turned off—
several times—
as my father and I would stand in the hallway
uncomfortably waiting for her,
fearful she would be hurt if we mentioned her ritual.
Such is the kindness shown to people we love.

Genesis 3:23: *So He drove out the man and stationed cherubim on the east side of the Garden of Eden, along with a whirling sword of flame to guard the way to the tree of life.*

Genesis 4:16: *Then Cain went out from the presence of the LORD, and settled in the land of Nod, east of Eden.*

Deficient Signage

Westward of Eden
we have lost our way.
We are naked in the void.
We await the work of later days.
We walk into nowhere,
my snake and I,
we are the perfect pair for an empty world.

This god has not provided to us the road map afforded others.
The Triple A has no information about this side of Eden.

About Me and God

On the Jewish holiday called the Day of Atonement
the fate of each person is fixed in a closing book.
Yet, piety and charity can change God's will,
or so it is said.
A benevolent deity would likely not presume
to reward or condemn without consultation,
but then again deities march to their own drummer.

I am spread-eagled on an alter in a distant place.
My heart is bleeding through my closed chest,
a wound not physical in nature,
while from the corner of the room I gather, through idle chatter,
that I am somewhere not my usual haunt.

God is everywhere so of course here,
indeed it is likely he/she/it
is the one which/who draped my bloodied body
on these altar stairs
and whose unerring aim
drains my body as casually as knitting.

I hasten to tell you what I have learned
as my life may be ebbing away;
you can know nothing, life being indiscriminate and the book
shut tight.

Lordy

I am not sure we are still on speaking terms, god and I.
She has surely made a mess of the world, and to blame it all on people seems to me too broad a generalization.
I thought god's work came with a warranty of workmanship.
We have had arguments, about this, although in candor they have been somewhat one-sided:
I have railed and remonstrated.
God has chosen her usual refuge in silence.

I have visited churches and temples and chapels and ashrams and mosques
in search of an explanation of this reticence to engage.
I have placed prominent advertisements, set in medieval fonts,
in the Christian Science Monitor and the Jerusalem Post.
I have placed a public service announcement in Al Jazeera in various languages.

Is one allowed to be angry with god?
Seemingly powerless to amend life by free will, what tools have we to contend?

In the words of Bob Dylan, with whom I am on speaking terms at least as successfully as I am with my god,
"if there's an original thought out there, I could use it right now."

Absolved

I am absolved,
absolved I tell you.
Not full-born from the head of Zeus,
but, mind you,
close enough.
Comes the sun of Spring
whispering of Summer
promising cleansing heat by sweat and travails unending,
but that is the false part of the promise
for everything ends.
So make best of what you have,
and of what is promised by glance and sound:
the birds in song, the sprouts in green,
the different winds stirring buds and shoots,
the tomorrow warmer still as if in confirmation.
And, by these things I am absolved, as promised by my God,
of all bonds I have made to that God
in foolish haste
in quaking fear
even yes is fervent belief.

And, I am absolved,
absolved I tell you,
by fire and pestilence abroad in the land
that kills the deserving
but has spared me
as sinners are spared even in the hour of judgment
(truth be told)
while the righteous who enjoy the thought of heaven
are rewarded for their wish.

And by reason of promises made to all
including me
I am spared each sunrise and each sunset
as I dare inhale the air and test myself,
that I should so prevail and be relieved
of all promises made to man
as men of righteousness shall fall
and those of sin do not deserve my adherence.
But, this absolution even my God denies me,
as he releases me from Him but not from Them.

And now one more work remains before the end of days
and this is harder still,
to seek absolution from myself.
Not God nor fire nor pestilence nor winter snows
that in my dotage chill my breast no matter the layers
of my defense
and turn my fingertips blue and numb even at height of day
will reach that stubborn deeply buried corner of my judgment
wherein I demand adherence to all oaths,
abjure all salvations,
deny all absolutions,
distrust all Valhallas
and even in the warm swathing of Spring
distrust all promises, despise all prophets,
reject all wisdom as merely true
but insufficient, because I demand
a person never conceived, or conceivable,
who fulfills all promises he promises his own self.

It is Spring, and hateful green of the grass is mocking me,
it avers I am a failure of mind and flesh,
I cannot even meet the dreams I dream,
lost in otiose reveries,
enchanted by obvious palliatives,
seduced by Gods self-served by absolution,
untorched by fire and pestilence,
left naked before the grass
which now I cannot see
as even prophets and truth are now denied.

I am not absolved.

VI

AGE

Annual Poem

Each year I will write a poem in honor of my age.
Each year I will ask why I am writing a poem in that cause.
Each year I will ask if the past year was a gift of one's
deity of choice
or of chromosomes
or of the medicine of our times.
Each year, I will ask:
How was last year?
Was I happy?
Or at least content?
Am I well, and what of others?
Am I richer or poorer?
Have friend and family passed, and if so,
am I sad for them, or merely
happy it did not happen to me?

What will I write when expectable agony looms?
When will I come to expect it?
They say nothing good lasts forever.
Will I stop then in my annual verse,
my markers on my roadway,
or will I write down my fears?
Or will I write down whom I blame?

Will I write when I am alone,
aged and bereft of family and friends?
It happens, you know—
some will have no one left to read their poem.
Will my book of poems end up trash,
scooped up by nameless people hired to clear out my room?
Will they pause to glance inside?

Cherchez L'homme

Are you looking for me, then?
About time.
Seems as if I fell down a dry well
and didn't make a splash.

Are those my clothes in a bag, dropped off at Goodwill?
Is some poor parolee about to wear my shoes?
Is that my stone being carved in the cemetery shop?
Are those my books being turned away at the library door?

So I'm glad you're looking for me, finally.
Because, as you suspect I'm still here.
In the air you breathe when you stand weeping in my room,
or in the flowers wilting on my pile of earth.

It is not enough to live just in your mind,
nor even in your heart.
I am desperate to be physical
even if only as left-over molecules in the dark.

Poor Goods Adrift

Liberation is not in your cards.
Your palm lines are indiscrete.
History indicts you constantly.
Your wide-eyed confusion is not endearing.

Is DNA your destiny?
Have you no will that's free?
Does it matter what you think you choose?
Are too many questions assailing you?

If you do not like the facts
and cannot answer these questions, either,
what, then, can be said of you
today, midst the flotsam of your age?

Why not just declare yourself:
Who are you, what you believe,
what you are willing to do
and what price you demand for the doing?

And, you ask, what if no one buys you on offer?
What if you are discounted in the marketplace of possible yous?
Were you too shoddy? Priced too high?
Do you lack some endorsement, and from whom?

A Depressed Man With Reason

His life
hung as a gray shroud around his shoulders,
stooping him under its weight
although the cloth itself was thin as gauze.

The pinch of skin in his neck showed pink
but his face was as gray as his garment,
suggesting that blood was pumping from nether parts
but dared not reach his face, to see and hear his fate.

His muse had explained it all to him
in terms so simple as to deny escape,
no exegesis to confuse,
no epiphany to excuse.

Legs propelled him straight, steady though with lurch
along a road insanely curved.
Guided by instincts he did not have,
no wonder he was treading in muddy ditches.

He had been born to promise.
No less a seer than his own mother had proclaimed.
He had been educated by the best of them.
They just were not good enough, it seems.
He tried to turn around but could not.
Seems he was already headed that way.

Who Goes There?

Who is that man
who walks with careful gait,
who holds handrails when walking down the stairs,
who leaves the party early to go to sleep,
who measures food and drink against next morning's schedule,
who dresses less smartly than before,
who begins to brush his teeth more slowly,
who walks with an interest in his surroundings
to facilitate his stops to catch his breath,
who stretches in the gym and gives up treadmills,
who smiles at younger women looking through and past him,
who brings his lunch from home,
who presses his flat palm on the shower wall,
who reads the obituary page each day,
who is offered seats on crowded trains,
who is called sir,
who has filled this page with questions,
who holds this mirror up with shaking hands?

Little Boxes

We are growing old together
And it is not always a pretty thing.

Seems from inside of me that each loss
Of power and desire
Seems proof I'm growing old.
Seen by you, I fear each loss of mine
Is an affront to you,
A personal insult marking loss of love.

I will put in two boxes all these things.
In one, the memories of what has been good.
In the other, the failures of today,
Where each failure demands to be categorized,
Placed in a particular continuum of anger,
Where each failure triggers in memory
The chain of similar failings past
And proves that nothing ever changes.

And these two boxes will be small
    and black
    and smooth-sided
    and with no way to reopen them.

We will call one "the good old days"
And the other we will call "today."
And each future day will relive each other "today"
And our lives will be the failures of today
Banging up against the memories of presumed better times.

And in this way we two shall grow old together
And it will not always be pretty.

(Published in *Ibbetson, Vol #46)*

STEPHEN M. HONIG is an attorney living in Newton, Massachusetts. This is his fourth book of poetry. His first collection, entitled *Messing Around With Words*, was followed by *Rail Head* and *Obligatory COVID Chapbook*.

www.ingramcontent.com/pod-product-compliance
Ingram Content Group UK Ltd.
Pitfield, Milton Keynes, MK11 3LW, UK
UKHW021036270726
13967UKWH00013B/2790